CAMBRIDGE LIBRARY COLLECTION

Books of enduring scholarly value

Cambridge

The city of Cambridge received its royal charter in 1201, having already
been home to Britons, Romans and Anglo-Saxons for many centuries.
Cambridge University was founded soon afterwards and celebrates its
octocentenary in 2009. This series explores the history and influence
of Cambridge as a centre of science, learning, and discovery, its
contributions to national and global politics and culture, and its
inevitable controversies and scandals.

Cambridge Jokes

James Orchard Halliwell-Phillipps (1820-89) was a Shakespeare
scholar, archaeologist and controversialist with wide antiquarian
interests. In 1842, while Librarian of Jesus College, Cambridge,
he published The Jokes of the Cambridge Coffee-Houses in the
Seventeenth Century, which he described as a collection of early
anecdotes 'selected from various Jest Books' which 'serve to show the
state of this class of literature during that period'. In this volume it is
paired with a pamphlet, The Fresher's Don't, written by 'A Sympathiser
(B.A.)', (probably A. J. Story) and first published in the 1890s. This
edition was printed in 1913 by Redin and Co. of Trinity Street (with
advertisements for Redin's and other Cambridge firms' goods and
services at the beginning and the end). This light-hearted guide to
student etiquette from the year before the cataclysm of the First World
War gives insights into a way of life which was about to vanish forever.

Cambridge University Press has long been a pioneer in the reissuing of out-of-print titles from its own backlist, producing digital reprints of books that are still sought after by scholars and students but could not be reprinted economically using traditional technology. The Cambridge Library Collection extends this activity to a wider range of books which are still of importance to researchers and professionals, either for the source material they contain, or as landmarks in the history of their academic discipline.

Drawing from the world-renowned collections in the Cambridge University Library, and guided by the advice of experts in each subject area, Cambridge University Press is using state-of-the-art scanning machines in its own Printing House to capture the content of each book selected for inclusion. The files are processed to give a consistently clear, crisp image, and the books finished to the high quality standard for which the Press is recognised around the world. The latest print-on-demand technology ensures that the books will remain available indefinitely, and that orders for single or multiple copies can quickly be supplied.

The Cambridge Library Collection will bring back to life books of enduring scholarly value across a wide range of disciplines in the humanities and social sciences and in science and technology.

Cambridge Jokes

From the Seventeenth to the Twentieth Century

J.O. HALLIWELL-PHILLIPPS
A.J. STOREY

CAMBRIDGE
UNIVERSITY PRESS

CAMBRIDGE UNIVERSITY PRESS

Cambridge New York Melbourne Madrid Cape Town Singapore São Paolo Delhi

Published in the United States of America by Cambridge University Press, New York

www.cambridge.org
Information on this title: www.cambridge.org/9781108001229

© in this compilation Cambridge University Press 2009

This edition first published 1842
This digitally printed version 2009

ISBN 978-1-108-00122-9

THE JOKES

OF THE

CAMBRIDGE COFFEE-HOUSES

IN THE

SEVENTEENTH CENTURY.

EDITED BY

JAMES ORCHARD HALLIWELL, Esq.

𝕮𝖆𝖒𝖇𝖗𝖎𝖉𝖌𝖊:

SOLD BY ALL THE BOOKSELLERS;

LONDON: TILT AND BOGUE, FLEET-STREET.

1842.

ADVERTISEMENT.

THE following collection of early Anecdotes has been selected from various Jest Books, either published at Cambridge or under the title of Cambridge Jest Books, printed in the seventeenth century. They serve to show the state of this class of literature during that period; and are also fair specimens of books that served in the place which our periodical literature has since supplied.

THE JOKES

OF

𝕿𝖍𝖊 𝕮𝖆𝖒𝖇𝖗𝖎𝖉𝖌𝖊 𝕮𝖔𝖋𝖋𝖊𝖊 = 𝕳𝖔𝖚𝖘𝖊𝖘.

A Draught Horse.

A scholar riding his horse hot into the water to drink, scarce up to the fetlock, one wished him to go in deeper, lest he foundered his horse. " Hang him, jade," says he, "let him drink up this first."

[This anecdote is printed by Mr. Thoms, from MS. Harl. 6395 of the seventeenth century. It is not in the first edition of Joe Miller's Jests, but has found its way into the more modern ones. See Thoms' Anecdotes and Traditions, p. 73, who remarks that " it might well pass for one of the Facetiæ of Hierocles." Not quite romantic enough, we think !]

The Growth of a Short Gown.

A master of a college seeing an undergraduate with a very short gown, reprehended him sharply, and told him it was a disparagement to the whole

B

society for him to go so ridiculously accoutred. "Good sir," replies he, "have patience a while, for it will be long enough, I'll warrant you, before I have another."

Very Small Beer.

A gentleman being in a place where there was wondrous small beer, said to his friend, "Oh, sir, this beer sweats extremely." "Your reason," said the other. "Why, I tell you, man, it's all in a water."

[Mr. Thoms prints an anecdote from MS. Harl. 6395, to nearly the same import:—"One remarked of very small beer, that it is but strong water at the best." The real joke is as follows:—A gentleman (?) applies at the bar of a beer-shop for a glass of beer, and, on remarking that it was very bad, the host exclaims that it was impossible, since it contained nothing but malt and hops; the gentleman ventured to add—"and a confounded lot of water." This is the tale as related in Derrick's jests.]

Plato's Year.

Two young philosophers went to an inn where the host was an old man, but very witty and conceited. They disputed there the greater part of the night, concerning the opinions of philosophers, especially of Plato's great year, how after thirty thousand years they should again be entertained in the same inn. At last they entreated the old man to wait for his reckoning until they came again after that period had elapsed, when they promised to pay him. To which he replied, " Thirty thousand years ago I remember you were here, and did not pay your reckoning : pay that now, and I will trust you for this until the next year."

A Cambridge Bull.

A student having a very small study, and having several friends in his sitting-room desiring to see it, told them, that if they all went in, it would not hold them.

A Clever Tale Teller.

A student having brought himself to a *non plus* in the telling of a tale, desired another to help him out. "No," quoth he, "you are out enough already."

The Aged Young Lady.

An old lady sitting at table with company who were questioning each other's age, being desirous to be thought younger than she was, said that she was but forty years old. A student who sat near observed, that it must be quite true, for he had heard her repeat the same for the last ten years.

The Industrious Tiler.

A tiler and his man were together at work upon a house, when the rafters breaking, his man fell down through the roof. The tiler looking after him, said, that he liked a man who would go through his work.

A Safe Sanctuary.

When there was a fear of invasion, some scholars in Cambridge were talking merrily how they would shift, and where they would hide themselves. " Well," says one, who was a bachelor, but who never appeared in St. Mary's, " you have provided for yourselves, but nobody takes care of me." " Yes, faith," says another, " I'll hide thee where I'll warrant thou shalt never be found." " Where's that ?" says he. " Why, in St. Mary's pulpit !" says the other; " the safest place for thee in the world,—for if ever any man looks for thee there, I'll be hanged."

[Printed by Mr. Thoms from MS. Harl. 6395.]

The Popish Minister.

In the time of Papistry, there was a certain man who, lying at the point of death, sent to the minister to bring the sacrament to him: the mi-

nister, being lazy, sent him back this sentence—
Crede quod habes, et habes! The man, however,
recovered his health, and borrowed the minister's
horse; and not sending him home again, caused
the parson to send for him, who received the
following answer:—

> Quod mihi dixisti
> De corpore Christi,
> Id tibi rescribo
> De tuo palfrido:—
>> *Crede quod habes, et habes!*

[From MS. Bib. Reg. 12 B, v.]

A Good Translation.

" Pistor erat quondam, laborando qui fregit collum:
  Qui fregit collum, collum fregitque suum."
Thus translated—
" There was a baker heretofore, with labour and
      great pain :
  Did break his neck, and break his neck, and
      break his neck again."

The Cambridge Townsman.

A townsman of Cambridge being in company
with students, and hearing them discourse, would

needs intermingle with them, and told them
that though they were students, yet could he tell
as well as any of them, what was Latin for any
part of a man's body. "Yea," says one of them;
"what is Latin for a townsman's head?" "A
head?" said he; and producing his almanac, looked
at the anatomy and said, "Why—ARIES, *head
and face:*" at which the company laughing, he
swore that if it were not *Aries,* it must be
Taurus.

[In old almanacs we find tables of the different parts of man's
body, and of the planets which govern them: so Aries governs
the head and face.]

A Good Translation.

A school-boy having to construe that line in
Terence, *Ventum erat ad Vestæ,* rendered it in
this manner—*ventum* the wind, *erat* was, *vestæ* in
the west: at which the school-master laughing,
said it was then time to hoist up sail, and immediately untrust the boy and trimmed his pinnace.

A Sensible Remark.

A scholar at dinner-time observed, that he
drank *once* as good beer as ever he did in his life.

The Witty Waterman.

A Cambridge scull being asked how he got so much wit, being but a scull, answered, where should the wit be but in the scull?

A Good Preacher.

A gentleman being at chapel, where a very dull sermon quickly dispersed the congregation, remarked that the clergyman had made a very *moving* sermon.

A Perplexity.

A young student told his tutor that he was very much perplexed, having been unable to find the Latin of the word *aqua vitæ* in his dictionary.

An Incipient Bachelor.

A scholar that was to take his degree of Bachelor of Arts, was asked by the Dean, who was to present him to the congregation, with what conscience he could swear him, who had spent his university career so unprofitably, to be fit for that degree both in learning and in manners? The scholar answered him, that he might well

swear him to be fit *tam moribus quam doctrina,*
for so the oath runs in the Latin.

Dr. Dod's Nephew.

One Dod, who was nephew to the celebrated
Hebrew scholar, John Dod, of Jesus college, went
up and down St. Paul's church-yard amongst the
booksellers, enquiring for *his uncle upon the com-
mandments.*

[Printed by Mr. Thoms from MS. Harl. 6395.]

The Latin for Cold.

A school-master asked one of his scholars in the
winter time, what was the Latin for cold. " Oh!
sir," answered the lad, " I forget at this moment,
although I have it at my fingers' ends."

A Noisy Undergraduate.

A fellow of a college was chiding an undergraduate for talking too loud at dinner-time, and
told him, moreover, that *vir sapit qui pauca
loquitur;* the other replies, " Yes, *vir loquitur
qui pauca sapit.*"

The Antiquarian Alderman.

A discreet alderman of Cambridge told some of his colleagues that they should overthrow the university in a law case, which was then in agitation, if, by searching the ancient records, they could prove Henry the Second to have reigned before Henry the First.

The One-Spur Horseman.

A student riding being jeered on the way for wearing but one spur, said that if one side of his horse went on, it was not likely that the other would stay behind.

[This is, no doubt, the original of the well-known passage in *Hudibras*—

"For Hudibras wore but one spur;
As wisely knowing, could he stir
To active trot one side of 's horse," &c.]

A Good Swimmer.

A foolish scholar having almost been drowned in his first attempt at swimming, vowed that he would never enter the water again until he was a complete master of the art.

[A similar story is told of a pedant by Hierocles.]

Almanac-Makers.

Two women scolding each other, one said, "Thou liest like a thief and a witch." The other replies, "But thou liest like an almanac-maker; for thou liest every day and all the year long."

A Handsome Man Asleep.

A foolish scholar, who thought himself very handsome, was at a party where a conversation arose on the change of appearance produced by sleep. "Nay, then," said he, starting up before the looking-glass, and shutting his eyes, "I will try then how I look when I am asleep."

[This tale is also told by Hierocles.]

The Scholar after Dinner.

A scholar of Trinity college, walking one day in the hall after dinner, was observed by one of the fellows to kick about some bones that he found there by accident. Whereupon the fellow asked him if he had dined? He replied, "Yes." "How comes it to pass, then," said the other, "that, the stomach being full, the bones are not at rest?"

The Complaisant Visitor.

A gentleman who was very tipsy, came to a friend's house, and told him that he had come three miles on purpose to sup with him : to which the other replied, that he was greatly obliged to him for coming so far to see him, before he came to himself.

A New Sign.

A drunken fellow coming by a shop, asked an apprentice boy what the sign was. He answered, that it was a sign he was drunk.

A Disappointed Bishop.

A bishop going to Rome to be cardinalized, was disappointed of his promotion, and returned; but caught a violent cold by the way. "It is no wonder," said one that was told of it, "since he went so far without his hat."

Ladies and Eggs.

One asked what was the reason that few women loved to eat eggs? It was answered, "Because they cannot endure to bear the *yoke*."

On a Man who Lost his Watch.

He that a watch will wear, thus he must do:
Pocket his watch, and watch his pocket too.

The Old Police.

A scholar, wondering why there were so many pickpockets about the streets, notwithstanding there was a watch at every corner, was answered, that it was all one, for a pickpocket would as gladly meet with a watch as anything else.

The Invalid Student.

An idle spendthrift, having nothing left to maintain his humour of good-fellowship but his bed, sold that; for which being reproved by some friends, he answered, that he could never be well so long as he kept his bed.

A Rambling Scholar.

One persuaded a scholar that was much given to rambling and going abroad, to sell his cushion, and it would be a means of making him sit harder to his study.

The World in the Moon.

It was asked by one, Why men should think there was a world in the moon? Another answered, " Because they are *lunatic.*"

[This anecdote was doubtlessly made in ridicule of Wilkins' book, entitled "A new world in the moon, with a discourse concerning the possibility of a passage thither," full of the most extravagant ideas.]

A Barbarous Trade.

One said that a tooth-drawer was an unconscionable trade; because his trade was nothing else, but to take away those things whereby every man gets his living.

An Unfortunate Lover.

It was asked by a scholar why Master Thomas Hawkins did not marry Miss Blagrove; he was answered, "He couldn't *master* her, so he *missed* her."

The Squinting Scholar.

One seeing a scholar that squinted very much; " Sure," said he, " this man must be more learned than his fellows, for with one cast of his eyes he can read both sides of the book at once."

c

Claret and the Gout.

A racketty scholar calling for a glass of claret, was told by his physician that it was not good for his gout. "What, my old friend, claret? Nay, give it me; for in spite of every doctor in the land, it shall never be said that I forsook my friend for my enemy."

A Bad Pun.

A countryman riding near a forest, asked a scholar who was by, what that wood was called. The scholar replied, "I *would* if I could."

The Greatest Wonder in the World.

The question being asked among solid persons, which were the greatest wonders in the world? it was answered, Women's and lawyers' tongues; for that they did always lie, yet never lie still.

A Bad Pair of Spectacles.

He that buys a horse in Smithfield, and does not look upon him with a pair of spectacles before he buys him, makes his horse and himself a pair of sorrowful spectacles for others to look at.

The Hen-Pecked Husband.

A citizen and his wife walking abroad in the fields, and passing by a large pond of water, amongst other discourse, "I would wish," quoth he, "that all the hen-pecked husbands in London were in the middle of this pond." "Sweetheart," quoth she, "can you swim?"

A Good Reason.

The reason being demanded why beggars stood in the streets begging with brooms in their hands? it was answered, Because they did with them sweep away the dirt out of people's sight; which, while they had a mind on, they would never part with a penny.

A Delicate Eater.

Two Bavarians were travelling together in Cambridgeshire, and by the way went into an inn and ate eggs for their dinner. After they were again gone forth on their journey, one of them said to the other, "I have deceived mine host very cunningly." "How?" said the other. He answered, "Because I ate a whole chicken in one of the eggs, and paid never a farthing for it."

A Bright Mirror.

A certain company of gentlemen were met together at dinner at a friend's house, where a boy was serving a pig's-head to the table in a dirty dish, for which his master did much chide him. One of the guests excused the boy, saying, that he was not to blame, for the dish was so clean that the boy could see his own face in it.

A Hint to Opium-Takers.

A gamester having lost all his money in a room where was one, with whom he had some small acquaintance, on a couch; he came to him, and said, " Sir, if you be not asleep, I pray thee lend me five shillings." The other answered, "Fast asleep, I protest."

The Complaisant Husband.

A gentleman, seeing his wife in a very sullen mood, asked her how she did. She answered him that she was not sick, nor yet very well. Nay, quoth he, then I may even turn thee out of doors, for I only promised to cherish thee "in sickness or health;" which answer awakened her sullen humour.

A Hint to Jack Ketch.

A hangman dealing somewhat rudely in fitting the halter about a Welshman's neck, he looked about very angrily upon him, saying, " Why, how now! what dost thou mean to throttle me?"

A good Description.

A country fellow having seen a gay lady in a pair of satin slippers, describing her attire to his companions, said that the upper-leather of her slippers was made of satin.

A considerate Barber.

A Welsh barber shaving a lean man, put his finger into his mouth to bend out his hollow cheek, that he might do it the more conveniently; but by neglect, cutting his own finger through the fellow's cheek, he gave him a great cuff on the ear, saying, " Confound your thin chops, thus to make me hurt my finger !"

A Gothamite.

A townsman going to sleep, put a brass pot under his head; and, because he found it too hard, he stuffed it with feathers and chaff. " Now," says he, " I shall sleep easy."

c 3

Lord Burghley.

The Lord Treasurer in the reign of Queen Elizabeth, advised her not to grant men's suits too hastily; "for," said he, "*bis dat qui cito dat,* —if you give so soon, they will come to you again."

A Miracle.

A person saying that it was a dangerous passage between England and Holland, was confirmed by another, who said that a friend of his came over from Holland into England, and was *drowned* by the way.

Be it known unto all men.

A young student not yet come of age, desired to be furnished with more money than he had allowed him. Whereupon he goes to a money-lender, who demands his bond, and he grants it conditionally that his father should not know of it. Upon this promise all things were concluded: but when he read at the commencement, *Noverint universi,* "Be it known unto all men," he cast away the bond and absolutely refused to sign it, saying, "If it be known to all men, how can it possibly be but it must come to my father's ears."

A Patent Stove.

A vagrant boy lying abroad in the street one winter's night, began crying " Fire ! Fire !" The people looked out of their windows, and asked " Where! where !" " I would I knew myself," quoth the boy, " for I would then go and warm myself."

An Epitomizing Historian.

One of our late abridgers of English history, in his work, said that George of Clarence was drowned in a rundlet of Malmsey ; and being asked by a gentleman why he agreed not with Stowe and others, who say that the Duke was drowned in a butt of that wine, he answered that in those great histories it might be called a butt, but that in his small epitome it might no way improperly be called a rundlet.

The Light Darkened.

One going in the dark, put forth his arms to prevent hurting himself, and running against a door hurt his nose. " Hey day!" says he, " I never thought that my nose was longer than my arms, but if ever I go in the dark again, I will not fail to take a candle in my hand."

A Conditional Letter.

A countryman writ a letter to a friend of his at London, after this manner: "After my hearty commendations, hoping in God that you are in good health, as I am at the making hereof, these are to let you understand that at this present I am extremely sick, and much troubled with an ague, insomuch that there is small hopes ever to be mine own man again. And although such a man hath done me most violent and dangerous wrongs, I do forgive him with all my heart and soul: but if it be that I may recover this sickness, I will be revenged of him to the utmost of my power, though it cost me all that ever I am or shall be worth. Thus being loth to trouble you any further, I remain your ever loving friend—J. F."

A Long Suit.

A gentleman sending for a tailor in great haste to make him a suit of clothes, told him he must make him a very strong suit that would last him a long while. A gentleman of the long-robe standing by, advised him to make a chancery suit, which he was sure would last him long enough.

A Man in his Cups.

A crowd having collected round a thief who had stolen a silver cup from a tavern, a gentleman near asked what was the matter. " Nothing," said a bystander, " save a man who has taken a cup too much." " Is that all?" replied the gentleman; " that may be an honest man's fault; and mine as soon as another's."

No Fun till I Come.

A thief was going to the gallows out of the town near Norwich, and many boys were running to see the execution; which he observing, called to them, saying, " Boys, you need not make so much haste, for there will be no fun till I come."

A Distressing Uncertainty.

A drunken fellow named John Thomson, driving his cart towards Wells, in Somersetshire, and being fast asleep in his cart, his two horses were stolen away. He awaking, thus soliloquized: " Either I am John Thomson, or not John Thomson. If I am John Thomson, then I have lost two horses; but if I am not John Thomson, then I have found a cart."

Good Latinity.

One thinking to put down a student with barba-
rous Latin, thus saluted him, " Ars tu fons?" *Art
thou well?* To whom he presently answered in
the other's garb, " Asinus fons asinus tu," *As well
as thou.*

Barren Assizes.

Two country fellows meeting at the assizes con-
versed on the news of the town, and one asked the
other how many criminals were condemned to
suffer. The other answered, " This hath been
the strangest session that ever was in my time; I
have not known the like, for there is no execution
at all: and is it not worth observation, that so
many justices should sit on the bench, and not
one thought worthy of being hanged?"

A Hundred Oysters.

An apprentice in the market asked the price of
a hundred oysters. A friend with him persuaded
him not to buy them, for they were too small.
"Too small!" replied the apprentice; "there is not
much loss in that, for I shall have the more to the
hundred."

A Fair Ghost.

A company of gossips were discoursing one evening on the walking of spirits, when, after a long discussion on the probabilities of their existence, one of them delivered her opinion thus : " For my part I have gone up and down all hours of the night, and yet I have never seen anything worse than myself; though, on my conscience, I think I saw the Devil once."

[From an imperfect jest-book in the possession of W. J. Thoms, Esq., but I am not certain that it forms one of the Cambridge series.]

The Well-bred Scholar.

One saw a man and his wife fighting : the people asked him why he did not part them. He answered, that he had " been better bred than to part man and wife."

Fast Riders.

Twelve scholars riding together, one of them said, " My masters, let us ride faster." " Why," quoth another, "methinks we ride a good pace ; I'll warrant it is four mile an hour." "Alas !" said the first, " what is four mile an hour amongst all us ?"

A Rebel Army.

Some scholars were sitting at a coffee-house together, and one was asking what news there were. One replied that forty thousand men had risen the day before; which made them all stare about, and ask him to what end they rose, and on what side. "Faith," says the informant, "for nothing I know of but to go to bed again."

[This jest refers to the extremely unsettled state of the country during the revolution.]

The Way of all Flesh.

A traveller reported to be drowned, a friend of his being in company when the letter came that brought the first news of his death, fetched a deep sigh, saying, " Peace be on his soul, for he is gone the way of all flesh." " Nay," said one near, " if he be drowned he is rather gone the way of all fish."

The Polite Scholar.

A scholar and a courtier meeting in the street, seemed to contest the wall. Says the courtier, " I do not use to give every coxcomb the wall." The scholar answered, " But I do, sir ;" and so passed by him.

Post Haste.

Mr. Field, the player, riding up Fleet-street at a great pace, a gentleman stopped him, and asked him what play was performed that day: he, being angry at so frivolous a demand, answered that it might be seen on every post. " I beg your pardon," said the gentleman, " I took you for a post, you rode so fast."

Epigram on Bambridge.

Good Mr. Bambridge, is now come to Cambridge,
  To speak de poles et axis;
He that brought him hither, may carrye him backe
    thether,
  And lerne him better syntaxis.

[From MS. Sloan. 1489, fol. 12, written in the year 1627.]

Receipt for a Termagant Wife.

The crab of the wood,
Is sauce very good
    For the crab of the sea:
The wood of the crab,
Is good for a drab,
    That will not her husband obey.

D

Homogenea and Heterogenea.

The boy who, coming to the university, heard them talk of *homogenea* and *heterogenea*, and not knowing what they meant, said, " Well, if I now were at *home again*, I would never come *hither again.*"

[From MS. Sloan. 1489, fol. 20, written in the year 1627. These words had not been long in common use at that period.]

A Good Woman.

A scholar once said to a woman who was complaining of him, " Be quiet, *bona mulier !*" at which, she being angry, the scholar answered, " Why, *bona* is good." " Well," said she, "if *bona* be good, then I am sure *mulier* is not."

[From the same manuscript.]

A Prayer for our Enemies.

Gurnet being asked why in St. Mary's he prayed for the mayor and the aldermen, who were so notorious for wickedness, said, " Because we are commanded to pray for our enemies."

[From the same manuscript. The jest itself is very poor, but is curious, as showing the state of feeling at the commencement of the seventeenth century.]

A Player's Retort.

Tarleton being upon the stage in a town where he expected civil attention to his prologue, and seeing no end of the hissing, he brake forth at last into this sarcastical taunt :—

" I lived not in the golden age,
    When Jason won the fleece ;
But now I am on Gotham's stage,
    Where fools do hiss like geese."

[From the same manuscript.]

An Old Adage Refuted.

A scholar having fallen into the hands of robbers was fastened to a tree, and left so nearly a whole day, till one came and unloosed him. " Now," says he, " the old adage must be false, which saith that the *tide* tarrieth for no man."

[From the same manuscript.]

A Good Similitude for Wind.

A man affirming that the wind might be seen, was asked what it was like. He answered, " It was like to have blown down his house."

[From the same manuscript.]

A Judge of Good Living.

A gentleman living in Cambridge a while, and not having his health, removed thence. Some years afterwards, coming to visit some friends at Cambridge, one of them chanced to say, " I see the place you live in now agrees better with you than Cambridge did." " Cambridge !" said he, " if I had lived in it till now, I should have been dead seven years since."

[From the same manuscript.]

A Hint for Genealogists.

Mr. More, who derived his pedigree from Noah, explained it in this manner :—" Noah had three sons, Shem, Ham, and one *more*."

[From the same manuscript.]

An Inveterate Jester.

A wit in Christ's College, Cambridge, playing upon another who sat at table, he at whom he jested shoved an empty platter to him, and bid him jest upon that. Whereupon the wit says, " It cannot be a bridle, because there is ne'er a bit in it."

[From the same manuscript.]

A Direct Answer.

A Staffordshire woman being asked what time
of the day it was, answered that the day was well
spent. She was again asked, " What is it o'clock ?"
She answered, " About milking time." " What
time do you milk at?" was the next question.
She answered, " Sometime sooner, sometime later,
as I can find time."

[From the same manuscript.]

A Satisfactory Permission.

A citizen newly made free, espied in Cheapside
a paper on a door, intimating that the house and
the shop was there to be let: whereupon he asked
a young man who stood at the next door, if the shop
might be let alone? who answered, " Yes, you
may let both shop and house alone, if you please."

[From the same manuscript.]

A Philosophical Reason.

A scholar was asked why a black hen laid a
white egg. He answered, " Unum contrarium ex-
pellit alterum."

[From the same manuscript.]

D 3

Good Comparisons.

By a preacher at St. Mary's. " This *dial* shows we must *die all;* yet notwithstanding *all houses* are turned into *ale houses,* our *paradise* into a *pair of dice,* our *marriage* into a *merry age,* our *matrimony* into a *matter of money,* our *divines* into *dry vines;* it was not so in the days of *Noe,* oh *no !"*

[From the same manuscript.]

A Dilemma.

Whilst a country parson was preaching, the chief of his parishioners sitting near the pulpit was fast asleep : whereupon he said, " Now, beloved friends, I am in a great strait; for if I speak too softly, those at the further end of the church can-not hear me ; and if I talk too loud, I shall wake the chief man in the parish."

Loan for Loan.

A scholar of Trinity College in Cambridge, having a chamber near another man's that was reputed a great scholar and had many books, some so rare as not to be had elsewhere ; the scholar

that laid under him going to this great scholar's
chamber, he desired him to let him see such a
book, which he did; and the book being in his
hands, he further desired to borrow it for some
short time, that he might read it in his own chamber. The other told him he did not use to lend
out his books, or let them go out of his own
chamber; but if he desired to read it, or peruse it
in his chamber at any time, it was at his service.
Not long after, the weather being very cold, and
the scholar that had the large library desiring to
have a good fire, and wanting a pair of bellows of
his own; and the other student, that would have
borrowed the book, having a good pair of bellows,
the great book-man sent to him, to pray him to
lend him his bellows: " I will with all my heart,"
said the other; and when he that came for them
thought to have carried up the bellows, he said to
him that came for them, " Truly I do not use to
part with my bellows out of my chamber, especially in such cold weather; but if you please to
come to my chamber, you shall have the use of
my bellows here, as much as you please, and when
you will."

[From MS. Sloan, 1757, fol. 10, written in the time of Charles
the Second. The same tale is told rather differently in MS. Sloan.
384.]

A Dangerous Generalization.

A tutor bidding one of his pupils, whose name was Charles Howl, to make some English verses, and seeing he put *teeth* to rhyme with *feet*, told him he was wrong there, as that was no proper rhyme. Charles answered, " You have often told me that H was no letter, and therefore this is good rhyme." His tutor said, " Take heed, Charles, of that evasion, for that will make you an *owl*."

[From MS. Sloan. 1489.]

A Bibliomaniac.

A dunce empty of learning, but full of good books, flouted a libraryless scholar thus, " Salve Doctor, sine libris." Next day the scholar going into this jester's library, crowded with books, said, " Salvete libri, sine doctore."

[From MS. Sloan. 1757.]

Tit for Tat.

A tapster bringing a can of beer to a gentleman, unmannerly blew the top off, whereupon the gentleman struck him a hard box on the ear, saying, " I do but give you blow for blow."

Little Heads hold Most.

A hot dispute happening among some merry
gentlemen, whether great heads or little heads had
the better wits ; one of the company said, " Without dispute little heads had the better, for it is a
maxim, that *omne majus continet in se minus,* the
greater contains the lesser."

A Considerate Mayor.

A country mayor being newly got into office,
that he might be seen to do something in it, would
persuade his brethren to have a new pair of gallows
built : but one of the aldermen said, that they had
an old pair which would serve well enough.
" Yea," said the mayor, " the old ones shall be to
hang strangers on, and the new pair for us and
our heirs for ever."

Quiet at Last.

A country fellow seeing a notorious mounte-
bank dead in his coffin, exclaimed, " Ah ! poor
fellow, thou art now still *for once in thy life-
time.*"

[From the same manuscript.]

A Merciful Castigator.

Two bedmakers belonging to a college in Cambridge, chancing to fall out in one of the chambers, the one of them struck the other with a fire-shovel, so that she desperately wounded her; and being blamed by a scholar for striking her with such a weapon, " Why," says she, "what fittinger weapon than the fire-shovel, for she is such a nasty jade as is not fit to be touched with a pair of tongs?"

[From MS. Sloan. 384.]

Oxford and Cambridge Actors.

King James had two comedies acted before him, the one at Cambridge, the other at Oxford; that at Cambridge was called *Ignoramus*, an ingenious thing, wherein one Mr. Sleep was a principal actor; that other at Oxford was but a dull piece, and therein Mr. Wake was a prime actor. Which made his Majesty merrily to say, that in Cambridge one sleep made him wake, and in Oxford one wake made him sleep.

[From the same manuscript. The play of *Ignoramus* is still preserved; see an excellent article on the Latin plays acted before the University of Cambridge in the new series of the *Retrospective Review*, written by the Rev. C. H. Hartshorne, M.A., F.S.A., of St. John's College.]

A Letter.

The following conclusion is taken from a letter written by a gentleman from Barnwell, near Cambridge, to a friend in London:—" If you be well 'tis well, keep you well; so farewell, from Barnwell."

[From MS. Sloan. 384.]

The Doctor Puzzled.

A gentleman who was very lame in one of his legs, without any outward show of anything, having sent for the surgeon, he, more honest than ordinary, told him it was in vain to meddle with it, for it was only old age that was the cause. "But why then," said the gentleman, "should not my other leg be as lame as this, seeing that the one is no older than the other?"

[From the same manuscript.]

A Thief.

A thief being seized as he was attempting to escape, very angrily asked why they held him so. "Marry," said one, "we only hold you for a thief."

[From the same manuscript.]

Cromwell.

One being asked whom it was that he judged to be the chiefest actor in the murder of the king, he answered in this short enigma or riddle:—

" The heart of the loaf, and the head of the spring,
Is the name of the man that murdered the king."

[From the same manuscript.]

Deeply Read.

A poet being deep in a shopkeeper's book, and demanded by him of money, he told him that he intended to dedicate his next book to him, and then the shopkeeper would be in his books as well as he was in his.

[From the same manuscript.]

New Way of Paying a Bill.

One going a shooting, would have borrowed some money of a friend. " Oh," says he, " what need have you of money? for if you have to pay any at any place, you may leave your gun to discharge your shot."

[Shot, or scot, is an old English term meaning reckoning or expence.]

Unused to Church Music.

A country wench going the matter of six miles to Cambridge market, chanced to pass by King's College Chapel at such time as the organs were going. She hearing the music went in, and seeing a seat empty, and being weary, sat down in it, which chanced to be the seat of the provost of the College, who being ready to come to the chapel, one of the officers belonging to it went to the wench and took her by the hand to pull her out, to whom the wench said, " I pray, sir, let me alone to sit still, for indeed I am so weary now, I cannot dance."

[From the same manuscript.]

Millers always had a Bad Name.

Two scholars passing by a windmill, stood for some time viewing it. The miller looking out of a little wicket seeing them, asked them what they would have, and what they stared at? " Why," says one of them, " we are looking at this thing, I pray what is it ? "Why," says the miller, "don't you see? where are your eyes ? it is a windmill." " We crave your mercy, sir," said the scholars, " we took it for a jail, seeing a thief look out of the window."

E

The Schoolboys Outwitted.

A schoolmaster in Christmas-time being shut out of his school by rebellious scholars, came to a composition with them, and thus subscribed the articles tended to him :—

" Æqua est conditio—non nego quod petitis." But being admitted into his house again, he called all his scholars to account for their rebellion; but they pleaded themselves, screened by the deed he had signed. He then calls for the original, and thus points it :—

" Æqua est conditio? non!—Nego quod petitis."

[From the same manuscript.]

An Optical Illusion.

A chandler having had some candles stolen, one bid him be of good cheer, "for in a short time," said he, "I am confident they will all come to light."

A Hint for the Americans.

A very sensible gentleman being asked how far distant in this age liberty was from licentiousness, replied, "Just as far distant as Norfolk is from Suffolk." "What do you mean by that?" said the other. "Why, sir, where one ends the other begins."

The Ruling Passion Strong in Death.

Two soldiers at Plymouth, being comrades, the one was an economical and the other a very extravagant fellow. The former falling very sick and weak, his companion one morning very early, for the sake of his money, takes him upon his back and was going to bury him; but, by chance, his captain met them, and says, "How now, Jack, what is that you have got on your back so early this morning?" "Why, my comrade," answered the fellow, "he is stone dead, and I am going to bury." With which the sick man cries out as well as he could, "I am not dead, indeed, noble Captain." "Oh," says the fellow, "don't believe him, Captain, don't believe him; for when he was alive, he was the hardenest lyingest rogue in all the whole company, and doubtless he is as bad now he is dead."

An Effective Police.

One having stolen a watch, the constable was sent after him, but without success. At last, being taken by others for a suspicious person, as they were examining him, the watch was taken out of his pocket. "What luck," says he, "to escape the constable, and be found out by the watch!"

The Baker and the Boy.

A boy being sent to a baker's for a twopenny loaf, complained that it was too little ; " Oh," said the baker, "it is the sooner eaten." The boy hereupon laid down six farthings and went his way, which the baker perceiving called after him, and told him there was but six farthings. " Oh ! baker," quoth the boy, " it is the sooner told."

[From the same Manuscript.]

The Lady who knew not herself.

Blind love had so bewitched an old doting knight that he married his cookmaid, one of a very low birth, and as ordinary beauty. Being thus translated from the kitchen to the parlour, one of her old friends came to visit her. She however took no notice of her visitor, only saying, " I am so far from knowing who you are, that I do not know who I am myself." Whereupon the woman said, " If you do not know who you are, I can tell you who you was ; you were Nan Dickley, old Dickley's daughter, and have gone many a Sunday about with me with a pitcher in your hands a begging of pottage."

[From the same Manuscript.]

Honesty of the Metropolis.

A country fellow sent on an errand from Covent Garden to Holborn, having his master's cloak
upon his arm, was loth to carry it so far, so hung
it upon the rails in Covent Garden, till he came
back; but when he returned, found the cloak
stolen. "How now, " says he, " I have hung my
coat five or six hours upon a hedge in our country, and the rogues never came, but I think they
are all thieves here in London."

Judge Jeffreys and Music.

When Jeffreys was recorder of London, some
musicians had a cause to be tried; but in the
midst of the evidence, he calls to the chief of
them, saying, " Well, you fiddler, what have you to
say?" At this the man was displeased, and said
he was a musician; upon which Jeffreys cried out,
" Pray you, sir, what difference is there between
a fiddler and a musician?" " As much," answered he, " as there is between a pair of bag-
pipes and a recorder."

[A recorder was a musical instrument very generally used in
the seventeenth century, and somewhat resembled a flute.—See
Hamlet, Act iii. Sc. 2.]

A deep Philosopher.

A gentleman riding down a steep hill, and being
afraid the foot of it was boggy, called out to a
clown that was by, and asked him if it was hard at
the bottom.   To whom the fellow replied, " Ay,
ay, 'tis very hard at the bottom, I'll warrant ye."
This answer encouraged him to ride to the bottom
of the hill, where he was presently immersed in a
very large bog; whereupon he called out to the
clown, " You country rogue, did not you tell me
it was hard at the bottom?"   The countryman
answered him,—" So I did, and so it is; but you
arn't at the bottom yet by a good way."

Comparative Misery.

One having an extreme bad cough, said, "If
one cough be so very troublesome, what would a
man do if he had twenty."

Wise overmuch.

Some gentlemen seeing a fellow stand still, and
it raineth very fast, they ask'd him why he stood
still in the rain?   " Why," says he, " you do not
think I am such a fool as to ride in the rain as
you do."

A Considerate Son.

A witch, being at the stake to be burnt, saw her son there, and desired him to give her some drink. " No, mother," said he, "it would do you wrong, for the drier you are, the better you will burn. "

[A few instances are on record of the burning of witches even as late as the seventeenth century.]

A Blind Man Illumined.

A gentleman had a blind harper playing before him until it was very late; at length he commanded his man to light him down stairs. The servant replied that the harper was blind. "Why, you ignorant loggerhead," says the master, "has not he the more need of light."

A Questionable Character.

Two men going from Shipton to Burford, and seeing a miller riding softly before 'em on his sacks, were resolved to abuse him. So they went one on each side, saying, "Come, tell us, master miller, art thou more knave or fool?" "Truly," said he, "I don't know which I am most; but I believe I am between both."

A Premature Wish.

One, meeting of his godson, ask'd him where he was going? " To school, sir," saith the boy, " That's well done," says he, " here is sixpence for thee, be a good boy : and I hope I shall live to hear thee preach my funeral sermon."

A Good Time.

One mockingly asked an astrologer if he could tell by his art when it was a good time. " Yes," said he, " it is a good time when a man is rid of the company of an impertinent babbler."

[From the same Manuscript.]

Nathaniel Field.

Nathaniel Field, the player, being in company with a certain nobleman who was distantly related to him, the latter asked the reason why they spelt their names differently; the nobleman's family spelling it Feild, and the player spelling it Field. " I cannot tell," answered the player, " except it be that my branch of the family were the first that knew how to spell."

[From the " New Cambridge Jester," 12mo. London. 1697. A somewhat similar tale has been fathered on Fielding, the celebrated novelist.]

The Poor Scholar.

One was begging, and said he was a poor scholar. Another told him he might teach children, which was better than begging. " Alas !" says he, " I am a *very* poor scholar, for I can neither write nor read."

The Fire of London.

One speaking of the fire of London, said Cannon street roared, Bread street was burnt to a crust, Crooked lane was burnt straight, Addle-Hill staggered, Creed lane would not believe it till it came, Distaff Lane had spun a fine thread, Ironmonger Lane was red hot, Seacoal Lane was burnt to a cinder, Soper Lane was in the suds, the Poultry was too much singed, Thames Street was dried up, Wood Street was burnt to ashes, Shoe Lane was burnt to boot, Snow Hill was melted down, Pudding Lane and Pye Corner were over baked."

[This is given with little variation in almost all the Jest Books of the time. It is worth preserving as an historical illustration.]

A Drowsy Cloak.

One Randall, seeing a friend wear a threadbare cloak, asked him if it was not sleepy? " Why do you ask," said the other. "Because," said he, "I think it has not had a nap these seven years."

An Ingenious Architect.

One seeing a great heap of stones in St. Paul's
Church-yard, said to a friend, " I wish I had some
of these stones at home." " Why, what would
you do with them?" said the other. " Why,"
says he, " I would build a *brick wall* round my
house with them."

Anecdote of Hobson, the Carrier.

A young maiden coming from Cambridge to
London to seek for a service along with old Hob-
son the carrier, being upon the road, he, among
other questions, ask'd her name ; she made answer
it was Joan. " Oh dear, Joan," says he, " you'll
never get a place in London with such a coarse
name. Your name must be Precilla, for that's a
fine name."

[This anecdote I insert from a little book, called " England's
Witty and Ingenious Jester." 12mo. London. 1692, p. 11. It re-
lates to an old favourite at Cambridge, and that is my reason for
inserting it here, for certainly it does not appear a very good jest,
although our ancestors may have thought it to be so.]

A Premature Desertion.

One being sentenced to die, fell on his knees
and besought the judge to spare his life, for the
sake of his widow and fatherless children.

A Mechanical Surgeon.

A valiant sailor, that had lost his leg formerly in the wars, was nevertheless, for his great prudence and courage, made captain of a ship; and being in the midst of an engagement, a cannon bullet took off his wooden supporter, so that he fell down. The seamen immediately called out for a surgeon. " Confound you all," said he, "no surgeon, no surgeon—a carpenter! a carpenter!"

Dr. Bentley and Boyle.

Dr. Bentley being in a very numerous company at Cambridge, after the election for parliament men a few years ago, was so elated on their having chosen two courtiers to represent the university, that he said " Now, God be praised, we've got rid of an old scab," meaning the candidates who were thrown out. To which a gentleman present replied; " Ah! Doctor, it is too true; but you will never get rid of a *Boyle* that you had some time ago, which will make you uneasy as long as you live."

[This anecdote is taken from a " New Edition" of Ben Jonson's Jests, printed at London about 1740, without date. It is curious as showing the general feeling of the time relative to the celebrated controversy between Bentley and Boyle.]

Example Better than Precept.

A father seeing his son doing mischief, cried out,
" Sirrah, did you ever see me do so when I was a
boy ?"

A Good Notion of Distance.

A Cambridge scholar, meeting a poor ignorant
peasant on the road, asked him how far it was to
Cambridge. " By my faith, master," says the
man, " I don't know, but from Cambridge to this
place it is counted seven miles."

A New Way to Pay Old Debts.

One Nash overtaking an extravagant young fellow who owed him a guinea, they happened to pass
by a village pound, when the lad threw a shilling
into it and bid Nash take that as payment of his
debt, *one pound one shilling.* " How now," says
the other, " is that the way you pay your creditors?
—a shilling in the pound ?"

Revenge is Sweet.

A servant being struck by his master, cried out,
" I am not certain whether he has killed me or no ;
but if I am dead, I shall be glad to hear the old
rogue was hanged for killing me."

A Specimen of University Etiquette.

A poor but witty youth, brought up in one of the colleges, could not afford the price of a pair of shoes, but when his old ones were worn out at the toes, had them capped with leather : whereupon his companions began to jeer him for so doing : " Why," said he, " don't you see they must be capped ? Are they not fellows ?"

Comfortable Assurance.

A gentleman that had occasion to rise early the next morning, bid his footman awake him at six o'clock. The lad, over vigilant, awaked him at four. " Well, how now," said his master, " what is it o'clock ?" " Four," replied the youth. " And why, sirrah," said he, " have you awaked me so soon ?" " Oh, sir," said he, " I came to tell you that you had two hours more to sleep."

Good Breeding.

A boy going through the streets with a loaf on his head, hit a gentleman with it accidentally, who thereupon began to abuse the boy. " Spare your breath," replied the youth, " I am as well *bred* as yourself."

The Use of the Solar System.

One saying in company how glorious and useful a body the sun was, another says, "The sun to be sure is a very fine body, but in mine opinion the moon is much more useful; for the moon affords us light in the night time, when we really want it; whereas we have the sun with us only in the day time, when we have no occasion for it."

A Dead Set.

The late Duke of Somerset having presented one of the colleges with a collection of pictures, a gentleman was desirous to see them, and for that purpose, asked one of the collegians where they were: to which he replied, looking about and pointing, "*Some are set* here, and *some are set* there, but where they really are set I know not."

Premature Ingenuity.

A young fellow, having been very extravagant, writ to his father for more money, and used all means, but nothing would prevail. At length he very ingeniously writ his father word he was dead, and desired him to send up money to pay for his burial.

Notions of Happiness.

" Were I but a king," said a country boy, " I would eat my fill of fat bacon, and swing upon a gate all day long."

A Solution of a Difficulty.

One lighting a candle, and striving to stick it in a candlestick, it often fell out of the socket, so that he grew very angry. " Why do you wonder?" said one who was present, "do not you see that it is light headed, and therefore cannot stand."

A Rent made Invisible.

A spruce fellow who was reduced in circumstances was asked by a companion, why he wore one of his silk stockings the wrong side outwards? " Forsooth," said he, "because it hath a hole on the other side."

A Polite Barber.

A wise barber having been to trim a doctor at night, was offered a candle to light himself down stairs: which having taken and lighted himself down, he brought up again, and returned thanks, and so went away in the dark.

A Participation in a Practical Joke.

Some unlucky lads in the University bearing a spite to the dean for his severity towards them, went secretly one night and daubed the rails of his staircase with tar. The dean coming down in the dark, dirtied his hands and coat very much with the tar; and, being greatly enraged, he resolved to make examination amongst all those that were most likely and suspected to do it : but chiefly he sent for one and laid it on him, as being most suspected to be the author. This the lad utterly denies : but the dean and the fellows being still more urgent upon him to confess the matter, he said, " Truly, I did it not; but if you please, I can tell you who had a hand in it." Here they thought to have found out the truth, and asked him who? The lad answered, " Your worship, sir ;" which caused him to be dismissed with great applause for his ingenuity.

[This is taken from a little book called " Cambridge Jests ; or, Witty Alarums for Melancholy Spirits," a copy of which is preserved in the Douce collection at Oxford. I have taken several jests from this book.]

Profitable Study.

" I read six hours every day," said a student of Catharine Hall, "and no one is the wiser."

An Easy Examination.

Two gentlemen meeting, saith one to the other,
" Would you believe that Mr. Drury being late at
Cambridge, had the courtesy done him to be made
Master of Arts?" To whom the other answered,
" Oh, yes, without a question."

[This is taken from " A banquet of jests, or change of cheare,"
12mo. Lond. 1639. A copy of this work is in the British Museum.]

The Living of a Musician.

One said that Dr. Wilson the musick-master,
when he first fell sick, look'd very thin. " Can you
wonder at that," said another, " when, cameleon
like, he lives by the air."

What is in a Name ?

When one talking of Sir Francis Drake's good
success, related how often he came home in safety
from so many long voyages. "Truly it is strange,"
said another, " that in all that time he was never
ducked.

A Good Idea of Magnitude.

One bid his shoemaker make one of his boots
bigger than the other. When the boots were
brought home, he angrily said, " How now, I bid
you make one bigger, and, instead of that, you
have made one less."

A Natural Uncertainty.

Two fools washing their feet in a brook, had so entangled their feet, that they knew not which was which; one would have this, the other thought 'twas his, and they began to quarrel. But a passenger seeing the simple contention, struck them over their backs with his stick, and fear soon made them find their legs.

Another Bull.

Two walking together in the fields, were at length hemmed in by a great ditch, which when they perceived, quoth one of them, " We must go back again, for this ditch is too big for us to jump over." " Nay," quoth the other, "I protest I'll jump over it, tho' I light just in the middle."

A Sudden Change.

One drinking some beer at a petty ale-house in the country, which was very strong of the hops and hardly any taste of the malt, was asked by the landlord if it was not well hopped. " Yes," answered he, "if it had hopped a little further, it would have hopped into the water."

Twin Brothers.

An Irishman was asked whether he or his brother were the eldest. "I am oldest," said he, "but if my brother lives three years longer, we shall be both of an age."

A Shallow Stream.

An Irish fellow in a bad state of health, applying at St. Bartholomew's hospital, told his physician, who examined him, that he had water in his head. "I suppose," said the doctor, "you have a swimming there." "Why aye, my dear honey," replied Teague, "so I have; but how could that be, if there was not water there?"

Medical Phrenology.

A lady complaining to Dr. Ratcliff of a violent pain in her head, he immediately pulled off her cap. "What do you mean, doctor?" said the lady. "I only want to feel whereabouts your pain is," answered he. "But you cannot feel it," said the lady. "Nay then," replied he, "if your pain is so very trifling that it cannot be felt, you have little occasion for my advice."

A Humane Irishman.

A jury being summoned to attend the coroner
of Middlesex to sit on the body of a woman who
had hanged herself, an Irishman going by, on seeing them enter the house, asked what was the
matter? And being told that they were going to
sit on the dead body, "Arrah now," said he, "then
I am afear'd if so many don't squeeze her to death."

Rate of Consumption.

One came into an inn, and asked the host how
long he had lived there?" "About three days sir,"
said he. "Then pray," said the other, "how
many barrels do you draw in a week?"

A Fine Child of its Age.

A country fellow coming to Blackwall, and seeing
the ships, asked one that stood by, what they were,
who told him they were ships. So pointing to one
of them, "Pray," said he, "how old is this one?"
They told him two years old. "How," says the
fellow, "and so big already! Why, what a huge
masty thing it will be by the time it is as old as
I am."

An Agreeable Correspondence.

A Welchman seeing his master tearing some letters, said, " Pray, sir, give me one, for I want to send it to my friends, for they have not heard from me a long while."

Characteristic Humility.

A tradesman newly made mayor of a little country town in Scotland, meeting with an old friend who spoke to him, and by accident kept his hat off, imagined it was done out of respect to his new dignity. Upon which, bridling and composing his muscles to great gravity, he said, "Put on your hat, sir, put on your hat, I am still but a man."

Mutual Assistance.

An old fellow of a college was pressed by some of the members to come into something that might redound to the good of their successors. At which he grew very peevish, and said, " We are always doing something for posterity, but I would fain see posterity do something for us."

[This anecdote is alluded to by Addison, in the Spectator, No. 583.]

Arion on a Dolphin's Back.

There was a spectacle presented to Queen Elizabeth upon the water, and amongst others Harry Goldingham was to represent Arion upon the Dolphin's backe, but finding his voice to be very hoarse and unpleasant when he came to performe it, he teares of his disguise and sweares he was none of Arion not he, but eene honest Harry Goldingham; which blunt discoverie pleas'd the Quene better than if it had gone through in the right way; yet he could order his voice to an instrument exceedingly well.

[From MS. Harl. 6395, and has been printed by Malone, and more recently by Mr. Thoms. Goldingham is stated by some to have been a native of Cambridge. It is very possible that Shakespeare may have had this anecdote in his recollection when he penned the discourse of the clowns at the rehearsal in ' A Midsummer Night's Dream.' The reader will recollect the passage to which we refer:—

" *Bot.* There are things in this comedy of *Pyramus and Thisbe* that will never please. First Pyramus must draw a sword to kill himself, which the ladies cannot abide. How answer you that?

" *Snout.* By 'rlakin, a parlous fear.

" *Star.* I believe we must leave the killing out, when all is done.

" *Bot.* Not a whit; I have a device to make all well. Write me a prologue; and let the prologue seem to say, we will do no harm with our swords; and that Pyramus is not killed indeed : and, for the more better assurance, tell them, that I Pyramus, am not Pyramus, but Bottom the weaver. This will put them out of fear."]

Honesty Rewarded.

A gentleman overtakes in the evening a plain
country fellow, and askt him how far it was to such
a town. "Ten miles, sir," says he. "It is not
possible," says the gentleman. "It is no less,"
says the fellow. "I tell you it was never counted
above five." "'Tis ten indeed, sir," says the fellow;
—and thus they were arguing *pro et con* a long
time. At last says the countryman to him, "I'll
tell you what I'll do, Sir, because you seem to be
an honest gentleman, and your horse is almost
tired : I will not stand with you, you shall have it
for five ; but, as I live, whosoever comes next shall
ride ten."

A-sleep and A-wake.

Anthony Sleep of Trinity, and Wake of Caius
College, used to have many encounters at the tavern;
but Wake never had the better at the wit unless he
had it at the wine, and then he used to cry out,
"O Tony, melior vigilantia somno."

[Printed in Thoms' Anecdotes and Traditions, p. 39. I have before given an anecdote (p. 34) relative to these two personages,
wherein it is stated that Wake acted before King James at Oxford.
Wake of Caius College represented two characters in the play of
Ignoramus, before the King at Cambridge, in the year 1615, and was
one of the "loving friends" to whom Ruggle, the author of that
comedy, bequeathed a ring.]

Advice Well Received.

Mr. Sleep, of Trinity College, being offered a small living in the country (of little better value than his fellowship) if he would leave the college; and advising at the tavern with his friend what to do, at last he sent for his horse and resolved to go to see it. But just as he was passing out of town, the sheriff of the county was coming, and his trumpeters sounded before him. Sleep turns his horse and home again presently to the tavern. His friends wondered at his quick return, and asked him the reason. " Why, in faith," says he, " as I was going out of town I heard a voice in the air cry, ' Tarry-tony—tarry-tony—tarry-tony ;' and away came I to my good fellowship again."

[To see the force of this jest, it must be remembered that Sleep's name was Anthony. This anecdote is also taken from Thoms Anecdotes and Traditions, p. 41.]

A Good Reason.

A certain minister going to visit one of his sick parishioners, asked him how he had rested during the night. " Oh, wondrous ill, sir," replied he, "for mine eyes have not come together these three nights." " What is the reason of that ?" said the other. " Alas ! sir," says he, " because my nose was betwixt them."

An Equitable Punishment.

Two scholars of the University, the one called
Pain, the other Culpeper, were both in fault, but
Pain was least to blame. When the fault came to
be censured, they were both sentenced to be ex-
pelled, but Culpeper, who was more to blame than
the other, escaped through the interest of his friends,
although the other was not pardoned. A Master
of Arts of another college coming to visit a friend
of his, asked what was the result of the business
between the two scholars, who answered him by
quoting the following line from Ovid—

Pœna perire potest, culpa perennis erit.

[This is taken from " A banquet of jests, or change of cheare,"
12mo. Lond. 1639. A copy of this work is in the British Museum.]

A Coffin in its Proper Place.

A master of one of the colleges having acted in
a tragedy, and his body lying seemingly dead upon
the stage—for the time was not yet come that he
should be taken away—a fit took him that he was
forced to cough so loud that it was heard by the
whole audience; at which, many of them laughing,
he excused it thus,—" You may see, gentlemen,
what it is to drink in one's porridge, for they shall
cough in their grave."

[From the same work.]

G

This is the Way Out.

A company of my acquaintance coming to an inn in Cambridge, and having remained somewhat long one of them desired the rest of the company to make haste, for they must be gone. " Why," said the host, "the best way to be gone is to drink hard."

[From the same work.]

Logic in Low Life.

Two Cambridge scholars meeting on the road with a Yorkshire ostler, they fell to bantering him, and told the fellow they would prove him to be either a horse or an ass. " Well," said the ostler, "and I will prove your saddle to be a mule." " How can that be?" said one of them. "Because," said the ostler, "it is something between a horse and an ass."

[From " London Jests," 12mo. Lond. 1692, in the Bodleian Library.]

Cut and Carve.

A nobleman being at a masquerade in a cook's habit, another person desired he would dress him a dish of veal cutlets. "Sir," said he, " you being the best looking calf in the company, I must cut the meat from your carcase."

A Merry Translator.

One said merrily, that "inter calicem supre-maque labra" was in English, betwixt Dover and Calice—the promontory of Dover being "Angliæ suprema labra."

Comparative Happiness.

Two falling out by the way as they travelled, began boxing, and at last they both fell into a ditch. A gentleman coming by says to them, "My friends, your falling out was pleasant, but your falling in much more so."

A New Road to Happiness.

A worthy doctor of Cambridge, among other charitable deeds, made a good causeway a mile in length at his own expense, to the great benefit of the country; and being there one day in person to visit the labourers, and to see how the work went forward, it happened that a certain nobleman riding that way by chance, and knowing him, gave him a kind salutation. But withal, thinking to jest with him, he says, "Master Doctor, notwithstanding all your great charge and pains, I should scarcely think that this is the highway to heaven." "I should think not," replied the Doctor, "for if it were, I should have much wondered to have met your Lordship here."

The Republic of Learning.

One asked another why learning was always called a republic? "Forsooth," quoth the other, "because scholars are so poor that they have not a sovereign amongst them."

[From the same book.]

A Boy not Born to be Drowned.

A scholar of Cambridge, in the time of the Assizes, seeing a boy in the castle-yard throwing stones at the gallows, said, "Have a care, sirrah, have a care you do not hit the mark."

[From the same book.]

Nature abhors a Vacuum.

A certain customer asking his barber where he might have some water to wash his hands, "Yonder," said he, "at the other end of the room you will find some in that empty tub."

[From the same book.]

A Glazier's Pun.

One complained much of the glazier, saying he was very unreasonable to ask so much for soder as two-pence a foot. "Truly," said he, "but you must recollect that it is always *so dear*."

[From the same book.]

A Wonderful Stroke of Wit.

Dutch Tompson of Cambridge being up very late at a taverne with other scollers, at last the clocke strucke one : "O dear," sayes one of them, "the clocke strikes one." "Why," sayes Tompson, "doe you wonder at that, it cannot strike lesse : drinke on, drinke on."

[From MS. Harl. 6395.]

The Beauteous Dawn of Day.

One having occasion to rise early, bid his man look out and see if it were day : the man reply'd it was dark. "Why then, fool," said he, "it is no wonder if thou canst not see—take a candle and hold it out of the window."

[From "Cambridge Jests," 12mo. Lond. 1674, in the Bodleian Library among Malone's books.]

Use is Second Nature.

A tailor that was ever accustomed to steal some of the cloth his customer brought, when he came one day to make himself a suit, stole half-a-yard. His wife perceiving it, asked the reason : "Oh," said he, "it is to keep my hands in use, lest at any time I should forget it."

[From the same book.]

G 3

Ringing the Changes.

One speaking of the wind said it was the most
changeable thing in the world, "for I went," says
he, "up Cheapside in the morning, and it was at
my back; and in less than half-an-hour afterwards,
when I returned, I found it in my face."

[From the same book.]

An Old Proverb Verified.

A carpenter passing by with a deal board on his
shoulder, hit a gentleman on the head with the
end of it, and then cried out, " Take care of the
board, sir." " Why," quoth the gentleman, " do
you intend to hit me again?"

[From the same book.]

The Effects of Galvanism anticipated.

A fool that owed a carpenter a shrewd good
turn, finding him one day in a sleep upon a form,
took the axe and cut off his head, and then came
into the house laughing. Whereof, when he was
asked the reason, he said, " It is to think how the
carpenter will look for his head when he wakes."

[From the same book.]

A Last Resource.

A witty, though unfortunate fellow, having tried all trades, but thriving at none, took the pot for his last refuge, and set up an alehouse with the sign of the shirt, writing under it " This is my last shift," which brought him much company and much profit.

[From the same book.]

A Gift for a Gift.

A Scotchman presented King James I. with a turnip of an extraordinary and prodigious size, which is a root the Scotchmen love very much. The King, pleased with the humour, gave him a hundred pounds, which another courtier seeing, if the King, thought he, reward a turnip-giver so liberally, what will he do to him that offers a greater present; and he thereupon presents the King with a very excellent race-horse: whereupon the King, turning to his nobles, said, "What shall we give this man?" And when all were silent, "By my soul, men," said he, "let us give him the turnip."

[From the same book.]

Sir Walter Raleigh served as well as the Pigs.

A lady of the west country gave a great enter-
tainment to most of the gentlemen thereabout,
and among others to Sir Walter Raleigh. This
lady, though otherwise a stately dame, was a
notable housewife, and in the morning early, she
called to one of her maids, and asked her if the
pigs were served. Sir Walter Raleigh's chamber
joined the lady's, so that he heard her. A little
before dinner, the lady coming down in great state
into a room full of gentlemen, as soon as Sir Walter
Raleigh set his eyes upon her, he said, "Madam,
are the pigs served?" The lady answered, "You
know best whether or no you have had your breakfast."

The Commons turned into a Common.

Lord Falkland, the author of the play called
'The Marriage Night,' was chosen when very
young to sit in the Parliament; and when he was
first elected, some of the members opposed his
admission, urging that he had not sown his wild
oats. "Then," replied he, "it will be the best
way in the world to sow them in this house,
where there are so many geese to pick them up."

In-door Relief.

A melting sermon being preached in a country church, all fell a-weeping but one man, who being asked why he did not weep with the rest, said, " O no, I belong to another parish."

A Prisoner Broken Loose.

Some thieves met a man, robbed him, and bound him in a wood. A little while afterwards they met with another, bound him also, and laid him on the other side of the hedge. Then one of them cried out, saying " I am undone, I am undone!" The other hearing him say this, entreated him that he would come and undo him also.

A Theatrical Anecdote.

A young fellow, who fancied himself a good player, resolved to take to the stage, and offered himself at Covent Garden Theatre; and having given a specimen of his capacity to Mr. Quin, he was asked if he had ever played any parts in comedy. The young fellow answered that he had played Abel in " The Alchymist." " I am rather of opinion," said Quin, " that you played Cain, for I am certain you must have murdered Abel."

NOTES.

———

P. 5, l. 7. *Quod mihi dixisti.* I find these lines given somewhat differently in MS. Sloan. 1489, in the British Museum, written in the time of James I. In that MS. they are as follows:—

> Nonne meministi
> Quod mihi dixisti
> De corpore Christi—
>   Crede quod edes et edis.
> Sic ego rescribo
> De tuo palfrido—
>   Crede quod habes et habes.

The tale is probably of considerable antiquity, for I find it alluded to in MS. Lansd. 762, of the time of Henry VII. There is an early notice of it also in *Grange's Garden*, 4to. Lond. 1577.

P. 25. *Epigram on Bambridge.* Since this was printed, I find the original of this satire in a MS. Rawl. Poet. 26, in the Bodleian library. It appears that Bambridge, or, as it is sometimes spelt Bainbridge, was chosen Mathematical Reader at Gresham College, and that the first public notice of his lecture was given out in the unfortunate form of a discourse *de polis et axis,*—a rich treat for the classical scholars of his university.

The Fresher's Don't

To the Freshers at Cambridge,
these Remarks and Hints are addressed
in all courtesy

BY

A SYMPATHISER, (B.A.)

SIXTEENTH EDITION.

PRICE 6ᴰ·

REDIN & Co., TRINITY STREET, CAMBRIDGE.
[Copyright.]

The Blue Boar Hotel,

TRINITY STREET, CAMBRIDGE.

The Most Convenient Centre for Visitors.

High-Class Cuisine.

Hot or Cold Luncheons served Daily.

Afternoon Teas.

Table d'Hôte Dinners.

GARAGE on PREMISES.

Telegrams—Blue Boar.   Telephone 303.

ARTHUR SHEPHERD

By
Appointment   *to* C.U.B.C.

the Best House for
BOATING & SPORTS KIT

SPECIALITY:
BLAZERS & FLANNELS

32 TRINITY STREET

CAMBRIDGE

The
Fresher's Don't

To the Freshers at Cambridge,
these Remarks and Hints are addressed
in all courtesy

BY

A SYMPATHISER, (B.A.)

SIXTEENTH EDITION.

REDIN & Co., TRINITY STREET, CAMBRIDGE.

AS TO DRESS.

Don't forget to cut the tassel of your cap just level with the board.   Only Graduates wear long tassels.

Don't wear knickerbockers with cap and gown, nor carry a stick or umbrella.   These are stock eccentricities of Fresherdom.

Don't wear your School cap in Cambridge, as 'Varsity and School fashions differ.

Don't wear School or other colours without being sure they are not identical with a 'Varsity or College club colour.

Don't aspire to Seniority by smashing your cap or tearing your gown, as you deceive no one.   Neither cut your gown, as it is not suited for a covert coat, and the style is not popular with the Dons.

Don't be a tuft-head.   The style is more favoured by errand-boys than gentlemen.

Don't continue the use of a beard, if you have acquired one since leaving school.   This excess of manhood is not popular in the 'Varsity.

Don't affect a hunting scarf or watch guard unless you really are a horseman.   Your friends will only laugh in their sleeves.

Don't by any chance sport a tall hat in Cambridge.   It will come to grief.

IN HALL.

Don't take seats which have been reserved, or attempt to sit at a boating or footer table for which you are unqualified.

Don't talk shop, or try to air you acquirements. It is most distressing to listen to a Fresher, who has just commenced the study of Chemistry, and who continually asks his friend : "To pass the H_2O," etc., or even worse to endure the conversation of a batch of well-meaning, and no doubt hard-working Freshers, who talk about nothing else but the knowledge they have gained to-day, and that which they hope to gain to-morrow.

Don't be continually enlarging on the eccentricities of your bedder, or the rascalities of your laundress. We all have bedders and laundresses.

Don't audibly criticise the menu or comment on its items, nor attempt to translate the remarks it contains. It will only appear that you are unaccustomed to dine out.

Don't joke with the waiters. They are apt to grow familiar if encouraged.

Don't forget that an occasional tip to the waiter will not be wasted.

IN YOUR ROOMS.

Don't " sport " during your first month. You will only earn the undesirable appellation of " Smug."

Don't attempt to make a palace of your rooms in the first week, as you will afterwards find that many of your purchases were not wanted.

Don't introduce tea-cosies or sugar-tongs, or you will regret it.

Don't neglect to offer tea in the afternoon, or coffee to evening visitors. You should also offer tobacco to all comers, whether you smoke yourself or not.

Don't play the piano all day, however accomplished you may be. It is not kind to your neighbours.

Don't attempt to keep every brand of wine under the sun. Most Undergrads cannot distinguish " Bordeaux " from " Burgundy " if served from a decanter.

Don't have business with touts of any description. The best tailors do not tout, and it is fatal to give an order to the man with " Our last series of engravings."

Don't, if you are poor, dole out tea and sugar to the bedder or landlady. They will soon find that you are not worth robbing.

Don't, if you are in lodgings, get too familiar with your landlady's daughter, as she is probably more clever than you. With other men's landlady's daughters you may be less particular, but even then—take care!

Don't forget to be courteous to your landlady. Many landladies have once held good positions, and if you are fortunate in having such an one, it is as well to respect her and not command. There is so much a landlady can, but need not do, and a little kindness will not be thrown away.

7
AS TO CONVERSATION.

Don't monopolise the conversation among second or third year men. They may cut you afterwards.

Don't, should you have left a Public School, air this fact before less fortunate Freshers. They will not appreciate it. nor like you the better.

Don't, if you played Footer for a small School, pose as an authority on the game, or talk too much of your prowess. If you are good this will show itself, and if not you appear foolish.

Don't, speak disrespectfully of a man "Who only got a third in his Trip, and so can't be very good." Before you go down your opinion will be "That a man must be rather good to take the Trip at all."

Don't, if you are aspiring to one of the three professions, attempt to pose as a K.C., a Specialist, or a Converter of Sinful Souls. The least informed people are usually most free with their information.

Don't speak with a provincial accent. It gives you away.

8

Don't repeat such jokes as the one about
  "We're all Christ's men here."   They are
  well-roasted chestnuts.

Don't, if you are from the Colonies, let it be
  obvious that your intention is "To show
  us something." We are not much behind
  you. Nor think that our fixed purpose is
  "To score off you." You often save us the
  trouble.

Don't forget that St. Peter's College is "Pot-
  house," Caius is "Keys," St. Catharine's is
  "Cats," Magdalene is "Maudlen," St. John's
  College Boat Club is "Lady Margaret," and
  a Science man is taking "Stinks."

Don't forget that Cambridge men "keep" and
  not "live."

AS TO
GENERAL CONDUCT.

Don't attend Chapel every day to commence with, or you will be expected to keep it up.

Don't cap the Master of your College, unless you have actually been introduced to him. Some Masters don't like Undergraduates. Neither cap all Dons, whether you have met them or not. You either irritate or flurry them.

Don't mistake a Don for a Gyp. The Gyp is the smarter individual.

Don't show contempt for the Deans. They are a well-meaning class, and very powerful.

Don't try to speak first or get up too frequently at your College Debating Society. You may be snubbed.

Don't attend all the meetings, or join all the Societies, to which you may be invited. Your future desertion will only cause worry and annoyance. Neither subscribe to every Mission or Philanthropy brought before your notice. There is no popularity to gain by this means.

Don't hang round other men's rooms for no purpose. You will get a bad name.

Otherwise and Everywhere.

———

Don't offer to shake hands. This is only done on the first and last occasion of seeing a man during the term. Tutors however are allowed to shake hands.

Don't leave your card on a Senior who may have called in your absence. It is your duty to call on him assiduously until you find him in.

Don't ask your Seniors to breakfast, etc., before they ask you, and never forget the respect due to Seniors, remembering that a Second Year man expects much more deference than a Third Year man.

Don't take the girl from the Tobacconist's or Confectioner's home. You gain nobody's respect by so doing, and the girl's only notion is to encourage a good customer.

Don't by any chance speak to girls without introduction. However innocent may be the motive, such practices are the worst distraction a student can foster. We know that it is only natural that a man should require ladies' society, and that if he cannot meet ladies in his own station of life he is driven into less desirable circles. We are also of opinion that the Dons, by arranging attractive "At Homes" and "Social Gatherings," could do a good deal to lessen a great evil ; but notwithstanding we strongly advise you — Don't make chance acquaintances.

Don't reply to a Boating Coach. His position is a very thankless one, and it is no wonder that he is occasionally irritable, or even mildly abusive.

Don't, should you be chosen to play Footer. shout about the field. This is the Captain's duty.

Don't forget your engagements. Nothing is more rude.

Don't be ready to think a man has cut you. Cambridge salutations are always distant.

Don't walk the streets as if you were part-proprietor of the Town. We have often been surprised to see Undergrads walking four-a-breast and jostling all comers, even ladies, into the gutter.

Don't, if you are a teetotaler, wear a blue ribbon. An obtruded virtue is almost as objectionable as a vice.

Don't be a rowdy or a drunken man. Rowdyism is more a badge of ill-breeding than of gentility.

Don't try to be a "Biood." These people are more despised than admired.

Don't live above your income. This only means worry and disgrace.

Don't buy dogs of itinerant vendors. They will not be thorough-breds. or if by any chance they are of value. they will be stolen dogs, and you will have irate former owners to square.

Don't attend Divine Service at the Pitt Press. The music is not good.

13
LASTLY.

Don't let your residence in Cambridge cause you
to assume superiority over others less fortunate.   The object of a University career is to
improve the mind by study and social inter-
course, so that the former School-boy may be
fitted for an honourable and useful career, for
the good of his country and the benefit of
those with whom he may come in contact in
after life.

CAMBRIDGE:
REDIN AND CO., TRINITY STREET.

College Notepaper and Envelopes

with Arms or College Address.

Paper with Private Arms, Crests, and Monograms stamped to order.

Steel Dies with Private Arms, Crests, Monograms, or Addresses cut to order. Designs submitted.

Visiting Card Plates

Engraved and Printed to order.

VISITING CARDS PRINTED FROM TYPE,

THE SAME DAY AS ORDERED.

Visiting Card and
Treasury Note Cases Combined

in a Large Variety of Leathers.

Redin & Company

Booksellers, Stationers, and Fine Art Dealers,

16, Trinity Street, Cambridge.

Printed in the United States
By Bookmasters